Soprano Teen's Edition

M000168477

THE SINGER'S MUSICAL THEATRE ANTHOLOGY

A collection of songs from musicals, categorized by voice type, in authentic settings, specifically selected for teens.

Compiled and Edited by Richard Walters

ISBN: 978-1-4234-7671-9

HAL•LEONARD®
CORPORATION
7777 W. BLUEMOUND RD. P.O. BOX 13819 MILWAUKEE, WI 53213

For all works contained herein:
Unauthorized copying, arranging, adapting, recording, Internet posting, public performance,
or other distribution of the printed music in this publication is an infringement of copyright.
Infringers are liable under the law.

Visit Hal Leonard Online at
www.halleonard.com

Foreword

Over the years several teachers have made requests to me for something just for teens in *The Singer's Musical Theatre Anthology* series. This volume attempts to address the needs of those teachers and their students. Another equally important factor in the genesis of this Teen's Edition has been the repeated experience of hearing young performers attempt to sing material that is unsuitable to them, both vocally and dramatically. There are no firm rules about what musical theatre literature is appropriate for teen singers, and individual talents certainly vary. Nevertheless, some reasonable guidelines were applied in the selection of material for the Teen's Edition, cited below.

The music should be vocally appropriate for a young voice.

To draw a parallel, in the study of classical voice young singers do not begin with dramatic arias by Wagner and Verdi. The same is true for theatre music. Most teenage sopranos would get into serious vocal trouble if they attempt to regularly sing music that is not essentially lyrical in nature. Songs that encourage more dramatic, big voiced singing, which can harm a still maturing vocal apparatus, have been avoided in this volume. As is the case with much theatre music for soprano, sometimes a combination of belting voice and "head voice" or soprano voice is used, depending on the song, range and context. For talents most suited to theatre music, this combination is vocally natural and encouraged.

The song and the role should be dramatically appropriate for a young performer.

"Appropriate for a young performer" does not mean that all the songs in this book are sung by teenage characters in the original show contexts, but if not, the characters are young adults. Some teens certainly attempt to play older character or dramatic roles at times, but generally, most young performers are most flattered by and most comfortable with songs written for young characters. Most of the songs in this book are sung by ingénue characters. A notable exception is "Children Will Listen," sung by the Witch then the entire cast in *Into the Woods*. Even so, the song seems perfectly appropriate and appealing to young singers.

The collection includes a variety of songs and styles, from classic to contemporary.

There is a common phenomenon of the young musical theatre enthusiast only interested in recent shows. Musical theatre has a vast, valuable heritage that needs to be explored. Additionally, young performers will only fully discover versatility as a singing actor by broadening their repertory to include classic songs from shows written in the middle decades of the 20th century.

Songs are presented in authentic editions.

Standard piano/vocal (or piano/vocal/guitar) sheet music has long been the general format for popular and theatre music. This format is very important for a song to find the widest possible uses, especially with millions of amateur pianists. But these simplified sheet music editions of show music, often transposed and with the melody in the piano part, are not the best source for a singing actor. *The Singer's Musical Theatre Anthology* series has always attempted to present the music as it was originally performed, with authentic accompaniment.

Songs are presented in the original keys.

Almost all songs in this Soprano collection are presented in original keys, with these exceptions:

The original key of "I'll Know" is just a bit high for many young voices. The transposed key in this collection should be more comfortable for teenage singers. The original keys on stage for Maria's songs from *The Sound of Music* were in a lower range, moved to a soprano range for the film version, and later for a Broadway revival as well. Though not original, the soprano keys seem firmly justified.

I appreciate and acknowledge Joel Boyd's participation in developing the Teen's Edition. I especially thank assistant editor Joshua Parman for his work on this four-volume series, and also his diligent help in the recording studio in creating the companion audio accompaniments.

Richard Walters
Editor

THE SINGER'S MUSICAL THEATRE ANTHOLOGY
Soprano Teen's Edition

Contents

ABOUT THE SHOWS

BEAUTY AND THE BEAST

MUSIC: Alan Menken
LYRICS: Howard Ashman and Tim Rice
BOOK: Linda Woolverton
FILM DIRECTORS: Gary Trousdale and Kirk Wise
FILM SCREENPLAY: Linda Woolverton and Roger Allers
FILM RELEASED: November 22, 1991, Walt Disney Pictures
BROADWAY DIRECTOR: Robert Jess Roth
BROADWAY CHOREOGRAPHER: Matt West
BROADWAY OPENING: April 18, 1994, New York; a run of 5,461 performances

Disney made its Broadway debut with a big-budget adaptation of its own 1991 Oscar-nominated musical film. Like the classic fairy tale on which it is based, *Beauty and the Beast* tells the story of a witch who transforms a haughty prince into a fearsome Beast (and his servants into household objects). The spell can be broken only when the prince learns how to love, and how to inspire love. Lyricist Ashman died in 1991 before the film was released. The stage score includes several songs written for the film but not used, plus five new songs with lyrics by Broadway veteran Tim Rice. Belle is a dreamy bookish ingénue, a bit of a social outcast in her own way. She receives a marriage proposal from the vain meathead Gaston. Belle is repulsed and reaffirms her commitment to explore the world away from her small town singing **"Belle (Reprise)."** When she discovers the Beast's castle after her father is captured and held prisoner there, she bravely offers to exchange herself for her father and soon finds herself adopted by the various living clocks, teapots, candlesticks, and cutlery who strive to match make their beastly boss and the eligible but understandably resistant maiden. Belle sings **"Home,"** added for the Broadway score, after first being imprisoned in the Beast's castle.

CAMELOT

MUSIC: Frederick Loewe
LYRICS AND BOOK: Alan Jay Lerner
DIRECTOR: Moss Hart
CHOREOGRAPHER: Hanya Holm
OPENED: December 3, 1960, New York; a run of 873 performances

Lerner and Loewe's first Broadway production following their spectacular hit, *My Fair Lady*, was another music based on a highly-esteemed work of British literature, T.H. White's *The Once and Future King*. The story is an opulently mounted retelling of the Arthurian legend, with its high-minded knights of the round table and its tragic romantic triangle involving King Arthur, his queen Guenevere, and his trusted knight, Sir Lancelot. Both Arthur and Guenevere are anxious about meeting each other for the first time. Near the top of the show, Arthur hides as Guenevere approaches the spot in the woods where he has gone to think. She nervously prays to her patron saint singing **"The Simple Joys of Maidenhood."** Just as her prayer ends, Arthur falls from his hiding place and their love story begins.

CAROUSEL

MUSIC: Richard Rodgers
LYRICS AND BOOK: Oscar Hammerstein II
DIRECTOR: Rouben Mamoulian
CHOREOGRAPHER: Agnes de Mille
OPENED: April 19, 1945, New York; a run of 890 performances

The collaborators of *Oklahoma!* chose Ferenc Molnár's play *Liliom* as the basis for their second show. Hammerstein shifted the original setting of Budapest to a late nineteenth century fishing village in New England. The two principal roles are Billy Bigelow, a shiftless carnival barker, and Julie Jordan, an ordinary factory worker. The score is rich with musical high points including **"If I Loved You,"** sung by Julie and Billy at their first meeting. Julie tells Billy that she has never had a boyfriend and will never marry. But her real romantic feelings, shown in the long musical lines of this song, contradict those declarations.

CINDERELLA
(television)

MUSIC: Richard Rodgers
LYRICS AND BOOK: Oscar Hammerstein II
DIRECTOR: Ralph Nelson
CHOREOGRAPHER: Jonathan Lucas
AIRED: March 31, 1957, CBS

Ever the innovators, Rodgers & Hammerstein were among the first to explore the new medium of television with a full-length original TV musical. The initial broadcast in 1957 starring Julie Andrews, drew the largest television audience to date of 107 million people. A new color television version was made in 1965, starring Lesley Ann Warren. The 1997 television film starred Brandy Norwood, with other songs by Rodgers interpolated into the score. Based on the fairy tale *Cinderella*, the musical follows the traditional story of a young woman who collaborates with her fairy godmother to overcome the plots of her evil stepmother and stepsisters so she can go to an extravagant ball and meet a handsome prince. Abused and underappreciated by her stepmother and stepsisters, Cinderella sits by the fireplace alone and sings **"In My Own Little Corner."** The fairy godmother magically appears and enables Cinderella to attend the royal ball. The Prince is captivated by her. In love at first sight, Cinderella and the Prince sing the waltz **"Ten Minutes Ago."**

THE ENCHANTRESS

MUSIC: Victor Herbert
LYRICS AND BOOK: Harry B. Smith
DIRECTOR: Frederick G. Latham
CHOREOGRAPHER: Fred A. Bishop
OPENED: October 19, 1911, New York; a run of 112 performances

The Irish born Victor Herbert (1859-1924) was the most successful American composer of his time. He and his mother moved to Germany in 1866 when she married a German physician. Victor received his musical training in that country and became an excellent cellist. Herbert's wife, a soprano, was engaged by the Metropolitan Opera, and he came along to New York, soon to be at the center of the city's musical life as a cellist and conductor. He began composing operettas in 1894 and wrote 40 such works in the next 30 years. The plots of these pieces are formulaic and often negligible. The only one performed regularly is *Babes in Toyland* (1903), although *The Red Mill* (1906) was successfully revived on Broadway in 1945 and was Herbert's biggest hit in his time.

EVENING PRIMROSE
(television)

MUSIC AND LYRICS: Stephen Sondheim
TELEPLAY: James Goldman
DIRECTOR: Paul Bogart
AIRED: November 11, 1966, ABC

The short-lived series *Stage 67* presented original teleplays, mostly by theatre writers in New York. Based on a John Collier story, *Evening Primrose* is about a poet who hides out in a department store to get away from the world. Much to his surprise, he meets hermits who have been hiding there for years, and among them is a young woman with whom he falls in love. She sings **"Take Me to the World"** after having heard about life outside the department store. Most of the music from this show was recorded by Bernadette Peters and Mandy Patinkin on his *Dress Casual* album.

THE FANTASTICKS

MUSIC: Harvey Schmidt
LYRICS AND BOOK: Tom Jones
DIRECTOR: Word Baker
OPENED: May 3, 1960, New York; a run of 17,162 performances

This fragile fantasy is concerned with the theme of seasonal rebirth, or the paradox of "why spring is born out of winter's laboring pain." In the story, adapted from Edmond Rostand's play, *Le Romanesques*, the fathers of two youthful lovers, Luisa and Matt, feel they must show parental disapproval to make sure that their progenies remain together. Luisa is forbidden to speak to Matt under the ruse that her father hates Matt's father, and sings **"Much More"** about what she wants out of life.

FIDDLER ON THE ROOF

MUSIC: Jerry Bock
LYRICS: Sheldon Harnick
BOOK: Joseph Steini
DIRECTOR AND CHOREOGRAPHER: Jerome Robbins
OPENED: September 22, 1964, New York; a run of 3,242 performances

An undeniable classic, *Fiddler on the Roof* takes a compassionate view of a Jewish community in Czarist Russia, where the people struggle to maintain their identity in the face of persecution. Based on tales by Sholom Aleichem, the plot is set in the village of Anatevka in 1905, and tells of the efforts of Tevye, his wife Golde, and their five daughters to survive. **"Matchmaker"** comes near the top of the show. Hodel and her sister Chava excitedly sing with another sister, Tzeitel, about finding a husband. After hearing Tzeitel's reply as she poses as the matchmaker, the girls realize that a marriage match might not be a happy one, and they backpedal on their wishes in the second verse. Tevye is deeply devoted to Jewish customs, and suffers as his daughters test this with their romances and marriage plans, disregarding the traditional role of the matchmaker. Hodel falls in love with radical revolutionary Perchick. He is arrested and sent to Siberia. The devoted Hodel explains to her father as she is leaving to join Perchik that she would rather be with him **"Far from the Home I Love."**

GUYS AND DOLLS

MUSIC AND LYRICS: Frank Loesser
BOOK: Abe Burrows and Jo Swerling
DIRECTOR: George S. Kaufman
CHOREOGRAPHER: Michael Kidd
OPENED: November 24, 1950, New York; a run of 1,200 performances

Populated by the hard-shelled but soft-centered characters who inhabit the world of writer Damon Runyon, this "Musical Fable of Broadway" tells the tale of how Miss Sarah Brown of the Save-a-Soul Mission saves the souls of assorted Times Square riff-raff while losing her heart to the smooth-talking gambler, Sky Masterson. **"I'll Know"** is sung as a duet by Sarah and Sky early in their acquaintance. The 1955 film version starred Frank Sinatra, Marlon Brando, Jean Simmons, and Vivian Blaine.

INTO THE WOODS

MUSIC AND LYRICS: Stephen Sondheim
BOOK AND DIRECTION: James Lapine
CHOREOGRAPHER: Lar Lubovitch
OPENED: November 5, 1987, New York; a run of 765 performances

Into the Woods brought together for the second time the Pulitzer Prize winning team of Lapine and Sondheim. After their first collaboration, *Sunday in the Park with George*, this time they turned to children's fairy tales as their subject. The book of *Into the Woods* often focuses on the darker, grotesque aspects of these stories, but by highlighting them, it touches on themes of interpersonal relationships, death, and what we pass onto our children. Act I begins with the familiar "once upon a time" stories, and masterfully interweaves the plots of Snow White, Little Red Ridinghood, Cinderella, Jack and the Beanstalk, a Baker and his Wife, and others. Act II concerns what happens *after* "happily ever after," as reality sets in, and the fairy tales plots dissolve into the more human stories. Cinderella evaded the prince earlier in the show. She sings of their second meeting, where she narrowly avoided capture by the prince **"On the Steps of the Palace."** At the end of the show, the Baker quietly tells his infant son the story of the boy's birth, and the morals we have all learned through the night of theatre. The Witch sings **"Children Will Listen"** (later joined by the ensemble). Though the role of the Witch is principally for a belter, "Children Will Listen" is in a more soprano range, thus suited to this volume.

JEKYLL & HYDE

MUSIC: Frank Wildhorn
LYRICSAND BOOK: Leslie Bricusse
DIRECTOR: Robin Phillips
CHOREOGRAPHER: Joey Pizzi
OPENED: April 28, 1997, New York; a run of 1,543 performances

The musical is based on Robert Louis Stevenson's 1886 novel *Dr. Jekyll and Mr. Hyde*. As in the book, a well-meaning scientist, Dr. Henry Jekyll, invents a potion that separates the noble side of man's nature from the evil, bestial side. Using himself as guinea pig, Jekyll soon finds he has unleashed an uncontrollable monster, Mr. Hyde, who cuts a murderous swath through London. Two women in his life help emphasize this difference: Hyde's scarlet-woman love, Lucy; and Jekyll's sweet innocent fiancée, Emma. In Act II, both Lucy and Emma air their conflicting feelings about their troubled men in **"In His Eyes,"** not realizing they are both singing about the same man.

THE KING AND I

MUSIC: Richard Rodgers
LYRICS AND BOOK: Oscar Hammerstein II
DIRECTOR: John Van Druten
CHOREOGRAPHER: Jerome Robbins
OPENED: March 29, 1951, New York; a run of 1,246 performances

Based on the novel *Anna and the King of Siam* by Margaret Langdon, the story takes place in Bangkok, Siam, early 1860s. Anna Leonowens is a young widowed teacher from England brought by the king to educate his many children. As Anna and her son Louis approach their new home, Louis confesses his anxiety at living in a new and unfamiliar environment. Anna reassures her son and herself by singing **"I Whistle a Happy Tune."** Tuptim, a young Burmese woman presented to the King as a gift, arrives escorted by courtier Lun Tha. The two have fallen in love on their journey but must continue their romance in secret to avoid the wrath of the king. They decide to escape and sing **"I Have Dreamed"** in anticipation of being together.

LES MISÉRABLES

MUSIC: Claude-Michel Schönberg
LYRICS: Herbert Kretzmer and Alain Boublil
BOOK: Claude-Michel Schönberg and Alain Boublil
ORIGINAL FRENCH TEXT: Alain Boublil and Jean-Marc Natel
DIRECTORS: Trevor Nunn and John Caird
CHOREOGRAPHER: Kate Flatt
OPENED: September, 1980, Paris; an initial run of 3 months
        October 8, 1985, London
        March 12, 1987, New York; a run of 6,680 performances

This quasi-operatic pop epic was one of the defining musicals of the 1980s, distilling the drama from the 1,200 page Victor Hugo novel of social injustice and the plight of the downtrodden (the "miserable ones" of the title). The original Parisian version contained only a few songs; many more were added when the show opened in London. Thus, most of the show's songs were originally performed in English. The plot is too rich to encapsulate, but centers on Jean Valjean, a prisoner sentenced to years of hard labor for stealing a loaf of bread for his starving family. He escapes and tries to start a new life, but soon finds himself pursued by the relentless policeman Javert. The pursuit continues for years, across a tapestry of early 19th century France that includes an armed uprising against the government, in which Valjean takes a heroic part. Along the way he acquires an adopted daughter, Cosette, who grows into womanhood and attracts the attention of the handsome revolutionary Marius, and the enmity of a rival, Eponine. The song **"In My Life"** gives Valjean and the young people a chance to wonder what each of them truly means to the other. It begins as Cosette's solo, presented here, before becoming an ensemble.

THE LIGHT IN THE PIAZZA

MUSIC AND LYRICS: Adam Guettel
BOOK: Craig Lucas
DIRECTOR: Bartlett Sher
CHOREOGRAPHER: Jonathan Butterell
OPENED: April 18, 2005, New York; a run of 504 performances

Finding inspiration in the same country as his grandfather's *Do I Hear a Waltz?*, Adam Guettel's *The Light in the Piazza* follows Americans abroad in Italy. The story, after a novella by Elizabeth Spencer, concerns a wealthy North Carolinian mother, Margaret Johnson and her beautiful childlike 26-year-old daughter Clara on an extended vacation in Florence and Rome in the summer of 1953. Soon after their arrival in Florence, through a chance encounter, Clara meets Fabrizio, a 20-year-old Italian man who speaks little English. Though there is a spark between them, Margaret protectively takes Clara away. As Clara strolls among the great art in the Uffizi Gallery, the paintings speak to her about herself, Italy, and her romantic yearnings as she sings **"The Beauty Is."** Fabrizio is determined, and with the help of his father, finally is able to spend time with Clara, though Margaret continues to discourage the romance. Margaret finally reveals the reason for her concern: due to being kicked in the head as a child by a pony, Clara has had arrested mental and emotional development. Margaret takes Clara to Rome to get her away from Fabrizio, but Clara's feelings for him remain fervent, and after much struggle she convinces her mother not to object to their marriage.

A LITTLE NIGHT MUSIC

MUSIC AND LYRICS: Stephen Sondheim
BOOK: Hugh Wheeler
DIRECTOR: Harold Prince
CHOREOGRAPHER: Patricia Birch
OPENED: February 25, 1973, New York; a run of 601 performances

Based on Ingmar Bergman's 1955 film, *Smiles of a Summer Night*, the score for *A Little Night Music* is composed in 3 (3/4, 3/8, 9/8, etc.), and contains Sondheim's biggest hit song. "Send in the Clowns." The show is a sophisticated look at a group of well-to-do Swedes in the early 20th century, among them a lawyer, Fredrik Egerman, his virginal child-bride, Ann, his former mistress, the actress Desirée Armfeldt, Desirée's current lover, the aristocratic Count Carl-Magnus Malcom, the count's suicidal wife, other guests, and some witty servants. Eventually, the proper partners are sorted out during a summer weekend party at the country house of Desirée's mother, a former concubine of European nobility. A film version, with a change of locale to Vienna, was released in 1978. **"The Glamorous Life,"** sung by Desirée's daughter, Fredrika, is an ensemble in the show; Sondheim adapted a solo version for the movie that appears in this volume.

LITTLE WOMEN

MUSIC: Jason Howland
LYRICS: Mindi Dickstein
BOOK: Allan Knee
DIRECTOR: Susan H. Schulman
CHOREOGRAPHER: Michael Lichtefeld
OPENED: January 23, 2005, New York; a run of 137 performances

The musical is based on the famous 19th century American novel by Louisa May Alcott about the close-knit March family of Concord, Massachusetts, during the Civil War. Four sisters (Jo, Meg, Amy, and Beth) and their mother (Marmee) make the best they can of their lives while the patriarch of the household is serving in the U.S. Army as a chaplain. Among several plot twists involving various sisters, Jo lands in New York, where she is an aspiring writer. She returns to Massachusetts when she hears that Beth, always weak, has contracted scarlet fever. Jo attends to her dying little sister. A still cheerful and peaceful Beth sings **"Some Things Are Meant to Be"** with her, eventually asking Jo to "let me go now." Though devastated, the family carries on after Beth's death. Amy marries Laurie, Jo's one time best friend who surprised her with a proposal she turned down. Jo matures as a young woman and a writer, and has a loving relationship with the older Professor Bhaer. The story ends with the announcement that Jo's book *Little Women*, about her life with her sisters, has found a publisher. There have been several non-musical films made of the story. The most often encountered are the 1933 film starring Katharine Hepburn, the 1949 film starring June Alyson and Elizabeth Taylor, and the 1994 film starring Winona Ryder, Susan Sarandon, and Christian Bale as Laurie.

THE MUSIC MAN

MUSIC, LYRICS, AND BOOK: Meredith Willson
DIRECTOR: Onna White
CHOREOGRAPHER: Morton Da Costa
OPENED: December 19, 1957, New York; a run of 1,375 performances

With *Music Man*, composer-lyricist-librettist Meredith Willson recaptured the innocent charm of the Middle America he knew growing up in Iowa. It is the Fourth of July, 1912, in River City, Iowa, and "Professor" Harold Hill, a traveling salesman of music instruments, has arrived to con the citizens into believing that he can teach the town's children how to play in a marching band. But instead of skipping town before the instruments arrive, he accidentally falls in love with librarian Marian Paroo. In Act I Marian gives a piano lesson to Amaryllis. Amaryllis, who has a secret crush on Marian's younger brother, laments that she has no love to whom to say goodnight. Marian comforts the girl and herself singing **"Goodnight, My Someone,"** dreaming of her own someone, who turns out to be none other than Harold Hill.

MY FAIR LADY

MUSIC: Frederick Loewe
LYRICS AND BOOK: Alan Jay Lerner
DIRECTOR: Moss Hart
CHOREOGRAPHER: Hanya Holm
OPENED: March 15, 1956, New York; a run of 2,717 performances

The most celebrated music of the 1950s began as an idea of Hungarian film producer Gabriel Pascal, who devoted the last two years of his life to trying to find writers to adapt George Bernard Shaw's play *Pygmalion*, into a stage musical. The team of Lerner and Loewe also saw the possibilities, particularly when the realized that they could use most of the original dialogue and simply expand or delete a few scenes. Shaw's concern with class distinction and his belief that barriers would fall if all Englishmen would learn to speak properly was conveyed through a story about Eliza Doolittle, a scruffy flower seller in Covent Garden. She speculates **"Wouldn't It Be Lovely?"** to enjoy the finer things in life. Professor Henry Higgins, a confirmed bachelor and linguist, makes a bet that he can pass Eliza off as a lady at the Embassy Ball. After months of elocution lessons, Eliza's studies pay off during an evening's study session. Excited by the success, teacher and student have an impromptu dance. Eliza reflects on the moment in **"I Could Have Danced All Night."** Once the bet is won, Eliza feels used and neglected. Eliza, now completely fed up with the professor's aloofness, demands a demonstration of love from her spineless admirer, Freddy, in **"Show Me."** Higgins and Eliza make peace in the end, and she returns to him.

110 IN THE SHADE

MUSIC: Harvey Schmidt
LYRICS: Tom Jones
BOOK: N. Richard Nash
DIRECTOR: Joseph Anthony
CHOREOGRAPHER: Agnes de Mille
OPENED: October 24, 1963, New York; a run of 330 performances

N. Richard Nash adapted his own play, *The Rainmaker*, for Schmidt and Jones' first Broadway musical, following their wildly successful *The Fantasticks* off Broadway. Nash's play is probably best remembered for the film version which starred Burt Lancaster and Katharine Hepburn. It is a simple tale of Lizzie, an aging, unmarried woman who lives with her father and brother on a drought-stricken ranch in the American west. Starbuck, a transient "rainmaker," comes on the scene and is soon seen to be the con man that he is, despite his dazzling charisma. He does, however, pay somewhat sincere attention to Lizzie, and awakens love and life in her. Nevertheless, she sees no future with Starbuck, and winds up with a reliable local suitor instead. **"Simple Little Things"** reveals Lizzie's true values, reflecting her no-nonsense, rural American upbringing.

THE PHANTOM OF THE OPERA

MUSIC: Andrew Lloyd Webber
LYRICS: Charles Hart, Richard Stilgoe
BOOK: Richard Stilgoe and Andrew Lloyd Webber
DIRECTOR: Harold Prince
CHOREOGRAPHER: Gillian Lynne
OPENED: October 9, 1986, London
          January 26, 1988, New York

The most financially successful musical in history is based on the French novel *Le Fantome de l'Opera*, published in 1911. It is the story of a disfigured musical genius who haunts the trackless catacombs beneath the Paris Opera. The world's revulsion at his outer ugliness twists the artist within. He conceives a passion for a lovely young singer, Christine Daaé, and hypnotizes her into becoming his student and worshipper. The Phantom's spell is broken with the arrival of a young man who vies with the Phantom for Christine's affections, and the Phantom turns murderous. The production's most famous element is a chandelier that falls from above the audience and crashes onto the stage. **"Think of Me"** is sung by Christine near the top of the show. It builds from a pretty melody sung at an audition, to the full operatic treatment on Christine's opening night, after replacing the ailing leading lady. **"Wishing You Were Somehow Here Again"** is Christine's plea at her father's grave, after the Phantom's threat begins to grow.

PLAIN AND FANCY

MUSIC: Albert Hague
LYRICS: Arnold B. Horwitt
BOOK: Joseph Stein and Will Glickman
DIRECTOR: Morton Da Costa
CHOREOGRAPHER: Helen Tamiris
OPENED: January 27, 1955, New York; a run of 461 performances

The setting of *Plain and Fancy* is Amish country in Pennsylvania, where two worldly New Yorkers have gone to sell a farm they inherited, but not before they have a chance to meet the God-fearing people and appreciate their simple but unyielding way of life. Farmer Jacob Yoder intends to buy the land from the New Yorkers and give it to his daughter Katie as a wedding present. Katie walks through the Pennsylvania countryside excited about her engagement and marvels at the world in "It Wonders Me."

SHOW BOAT

MUSIC: Jerome Kern
LYRICS AND BOOK: Oscar Hammerstein II
DIRECTORS: Zeke Colvan and Oscar Hammerstein II
CHOREOGRAPHER: Sammy Lee
OPENED: December 27, 1927, New York; a run of 572 performances

No show ever to hit Broadway was more historically important, and at the same time more beloved than *Show Boat*, that landmark of the 1927 season. Edna Ferber's novel of life on the Mississippi was the source for this musical/operetta, and provided a rich plot and characters which Kern and Hammerstein amplified to become some of the most memorable ever to grace the stage. *Show Boat* not only summed up all that had come before it, both in the musical and operetta genres, and in a distinctly American style, but additionally planted a seed of complete congruity which would later blossom in the more adventurous shows of the 1930s, '40s, and '50s. At their first meeting Ravenal mistakenly things Magnolia is an actress; she is not (yet), but is happy to **"Make Believe"** with him. There are two film versions, released in 1936 and 1951.

THE SOUND OF MUSIC

MUSIC: Richard Rodgers
LYRICS: Oscar Hammerstein II
BOOK: Howard Lindsay and Russel Crouse
DIRECTOR: Vincent J. Donehue
CHOREOGRAPHER: Joe Layton
OPENED: November 16, 1959, New York; a run of 1,443 performances

The Sound of Music was adapted from Maria von Trapp's autobiographical *The Trapp Family Singers*. It is set in Austria in 1938 during the Anschluss (The Nazi annexation of Austria to Germany). As the show opens, Maria Rainer, a free-spirited postulant at Nonnburg Abbey sings **"The Sound of Music,"** in love with the Alpine nature. She takes a position as governess to the seven children of the widowed and autocratic Captain Georg von Trapp. Maria loosens things up around the house, which has been run like a battleship since the death of the children's mother, teaching the children to sing and play, and thereby melting the Captain's heart. After Maria and the Captain marry, the family flees over the Alps into Switzerland to escape the Nazis. **"My Favorite Things"** is sung in the stage show by Maria and the Mother Abbess to give Maria courage. In the film, Maria sings the tune to the children to comfort them during a thunderstorm. After Hammerstein's death from cancer, Rodgers wrote both music and lyrics for two songs that were added to the film: **"I Have Confidence,"** a song for Maria as she heads for her first day as governess, and "Something Good," and intimate love song for the Captain and Maria once they accept their feelings for one another. The stage score, written for the modest range of Mary Martin, was transposed into a soprano range for the film and 1998 Broadway revival.

SPRING AWAKENING

MUSIC: Duncan Sheik
LYRICS AND BOOK: Steven Sater
DIRECTOR: Michael Mayer
CHOREOGRAPHER: Bill T. Jones
OPENED: December 10, 2006, New York; a run of 859 performances

This rock musical, 2007 Tony Award winner of Best Musical, is based on the 1891 German play by Frank Wedekind, which was banned for decades because of its frankness about teenage sex and suicide. The setting is a provincial German town in the 1890s. Teenagers struggle against strict morals of adults and the lack of instruction and communication about sex and emotion. Wendla Bergmann is a girl discovering her sexuality and sensuality in a time that forbids such things. By chance she meets Melchior in a secluded forest and they surrender to their desires. Melchior's friend Mortiz is so distraught that he kills himself; the headmasters of the blame Melchior and expel him. Meanwhile, Wendla has become pregnant. In Act II, Wendla sings the ponderous **"Whispering"** about her difficult predicament. Though the range of the song is limited, the original cast recording demonstrates that it is for an amplified rock soprano timbre, not a theatre belting voice. Wendla's mother finds someone who will perform an abortion in secret, but Wendla dies as a result of it, though officially her death is attributed to anemia. Melchior considers suicide, but the spirits of Wendla and Moritz comfort him and he continues on.

SWEENEY TODD, THE DEMON BARBER OF FLEET STREET

MUSIC AND LYRICS: Stephen Sondheim
BOOK: Hugh Wheeler
DIRECTOR: Harold Prince
CHOREOGRAPHER: Larry Fuller
OPENED: March 1, 1979, New York; a run of 557 performances

Despite the sordidness of its main plot—a half mad, vengeance-obsessed barber in Victorian London slits the throats of his customers whose corpses are then turned into meat pies by his accomplice, Mrs. Lovett—this near-operatic musical is a bold and brilliant depiction of the cannibalizing effects of the Industrial Revolution. Sweeney Todd first appeared on the London stage in 1842 in a play called *A String of Pearls, or The Fiend of Fleet Street*. Other versions followed, the most recent being Christopher Bond's *Sweeney Todd*, produced in 1973, which served as the basis of the musical. Johanna is under the care of the scheming Judge Turpin, who years earlier, had Todd exiled on a trumped up charge in order to steal his wife. Johann (Todd's daughter) notices a vendor selling caged birds from her window and, feeling entrapped herself, sings her entrance song, **"Green Finch and Linnet Bird."**

WEST SIDE STORY

MUSIC: Leonard Bernstein
LYRICS: Stephen Sondheim
BOOK: Arthur Laurents
DIRECTOR: Jerome Robbins
CHOREOGRAPHERS: Jerome Robbins and Peter Gennaro
OPENED: September 26, 1957, New York; a run of 732 performances

West Side Story is loosely based on Williams Shakespeare's *Romeo and Juliet*. Gangs rule the streets of the west side of New York City in the 1950s, before the area was revitalized with the construction of Lincoln Center in the 1960s. The Jets are tough Americans in hate-filled rivalry with the Sharks. Tony, a former Jet trying to go straight with a regular job, meets Maria, sister to one of the Sharks, at a dance. They instantly fall in love, drawing anger from Maria's brother, Bernardo, leader of the Sharks. Riff, leader of the Jets, challenges the Sharks to a rumble. Tony later secretly visits Maria's fire escape balcony, where they confirm their love, uniting as one the next day, after business hours, in the bridal shop where Maria works. That evening Tony goes to the rumble to try to stop it, but when Bernardo stabs Riff, Tony instinctively stabs and kills Bernardo. As this is happening, before she knows of her brother's death, in her bedroom Maria confesses to her friends her emotions at being in love in **"I Feel Pretty,"** which opens ACT II. The 1961 film version retained most of the score, but made significant shifts in songs and scene order.

WICKED

MUSIC AND LYRICS: Stephen Schwartz
BOOK: Winnie Holzman
DIRECTOR: Joe Mantello
CHOREOGRAPHER: Wayne Cilento
OPENED: October 30, 2003

Based on Gregory Maguir's 1995 book, *Wicked* chronicles the back story of the Wicked Witch of the West, Elphaba, and Good Witch of the North, Glinda (Galinda), before their story threads are picked up in L. Frank Baum's *The Wonderful Wizard of Oz*. The two witches first cross paths in school as unlikely roommates. Elphaba, shy and green, learns from radiant Galinda just what it takes to be **"Popular."**

WONDERFUL TOWN

MUSIC: Leonard Bernstein
LYRICS: Betty Comden and Adolph Green
BOOK: Joseph A. Fields and Jerome Chodorov
DIRECTOR: George Abbott
CHOREOGRAPHER: Donald Saddler
OPENED: February 25, 1953, New York; a run of 559 performances

Set in New York, *Wonderful Town* is based on the hit Broadway play *My Sister Eileen*, which itself was based on Ruth McKinney's semi-autobiographical *New Yorker* short stories. Ruth and Eileen are two sisters making their way in Greenwich Village, originally from a small town in Ohio. Ruth is a writer, and Eileen is . . . well, pretty. As Ruth chases the story, Eileen is chased by suitor after suitor. Ruth's editor, Bob Baker, comes over to apologize for being curt with Ruth, and Eileen immediately falls **"A Little Bit in Love"** with him. After a raucous night with seven amorous, Conga-dancing Brazilian naval cadets that lands Eileen in jail, all is well in the end as she realizes that Ruth and Bob love one another, and Eileen finds a singing career.

BELLE
(Reprise)
from Walt Disney's *Beauty and the Beast*

Lyrics by HOWARD ASHMAN
Music by ALAN MENKEN

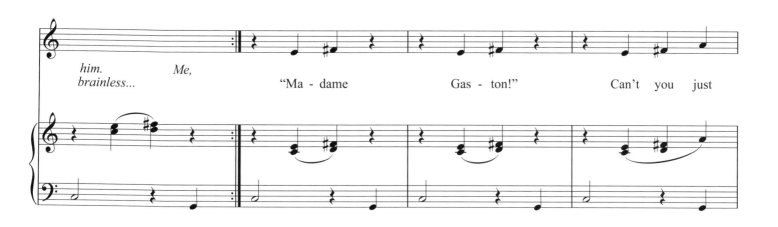

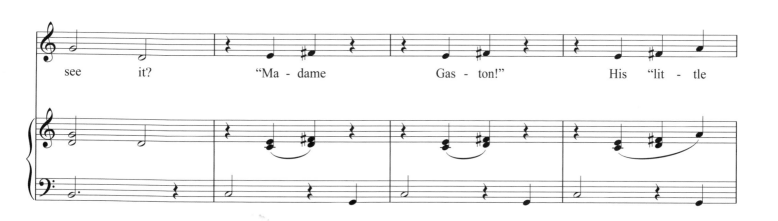

© 1991 Walt Disney Music Company and Wonderland Music Company, Inc.
All Rights Reserved   Used by Permission

wife." No, sir. Not me! I guar - an -

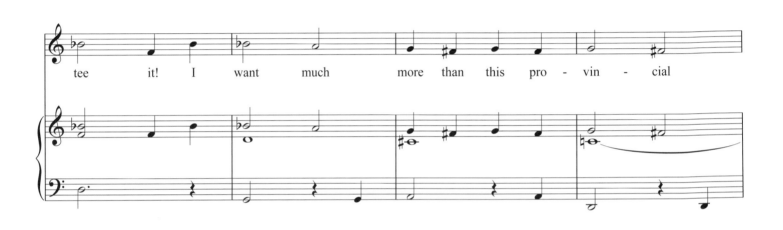

tee it! I want much more than this pro - vin - cial

life.

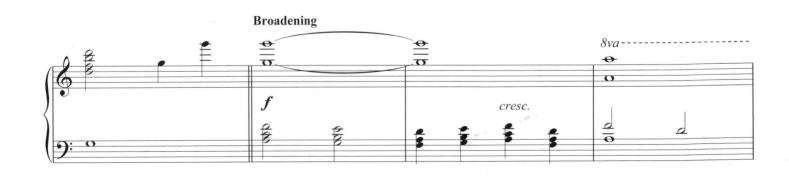

HOME
from Walt Disney's *Beauty and the Beast: The Broadway Musical*

Music by ALAN MENKEN
Lyrics by TIM RICE

Yes, I made the choice. For Pa - pa, I will stay.

But I don't de - serve to lose my free - dom in this way, you mon - ster! ____

____ If you think that what you've done ____ is right, well

© 1994 Wonderland Music Company, Inc., Menken Music, Trunksong Music Ltd. and Walt Disney Music Company
All Rights Reserved Used by Permission

THE SIMPLE JOYS OF MAIDENHOOD
from *Camelot*

Words by ALAN JAY LERNER
Music by FREDERICK LOEWE

Animato molto

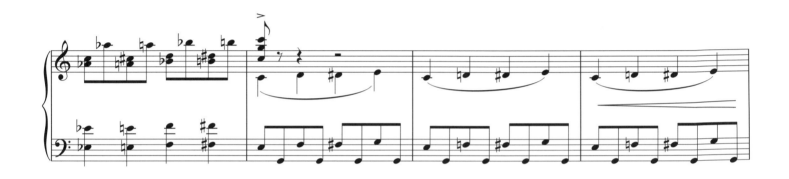

Copyright © 1960, 1961 by Alan Jay Lerner and Frederick Loewe
Copyright Renewed
Chappell & Co., owner of publication and allied rights throughout the world
International Copyright Secured   All Rights Reserved

Allegro
(with vehement rebellion)

won't o - bey you an - y - more! You've gone a bit too far. I won't be bid and

bar - gain'd for Like beads at a ba - zaar. St. Gen - e - vieve, I've run a - way, E -

lud - ed them and fled, And from now on I in - tend to pray to some - one else in -

stead.

Moderato
(plaintively)

Oh, Gen - e - vieve! St. Gen - e - vieve! Where were you when my youth was

sold? Dear Gen - e - vieve, sweet Gen - e - vieve, Shan't I be young be - fore I'm

Allegro

*Optional cut to ** *

old?

Shan't I, St. Genevieve?   *Why must I suffer this squalid destiny?*   *Just when I reach the*

golden age of eligibility and wooability. Is my fate determined by love and courtship?

Oh, no. Clause one: fix the border; Clause two: establish trade;

rall.

rall.

Poco meno mosso

Clause three: deliver me; Clause four: stop the war; five, six: pick up sticks. How cruel! How

rall.

unjust! Am I never to know the joys of maidenhood? The conventional, ordinary, garden variety joys of maidenhood?

poco rall.

rall.

**If the cut is taken the spoken lines are omitted.

Allegretto

pp

Where are the sim - ple joys of maid - en - hood? _____ Where are

all those a - dor - ing, dar - ling boys? _____ Where's the

knight pin - ing so for me He leaps to death in woe for me? Oh,

where are a maid - en's sim - ple joys? _____ Shan't

I have the nor - mal life a maid - en should?_____ Shall I

nev - er be res - cued in the wood?_____ Shall two

knights nev - er tilt for me And let their blood be spilt for me? Oh,

where are the sim - ple joys of maid - en - hood?

Shall I not be on a ped-es-tal, Wor-shipped and com-pet-ed for?

Not be car-ried off, or bet-ter still, Cause a lit-tle war?

poco rall.

a tempo

Where are the sim-ple joys of maid-en-hood?_____ Are those

sweet, gen-tle pleas-ures gone for good?_____ Shall a

feud not be - gin for me? Shall kith not kill their kin for me? Oh,

where are the triv - ial joys...? Harm - less, con - viv - ial joys...?

Where are the sim - ple joys of maid - en -

poco rall.

Poco più mosso

hood? _____

IN MY OWN LITTLE CORNER

from *Cinderella*

Lyrics by OSCAR HAMMERSTEIN II
Music by RICHARD RODGERS

Ben moderato

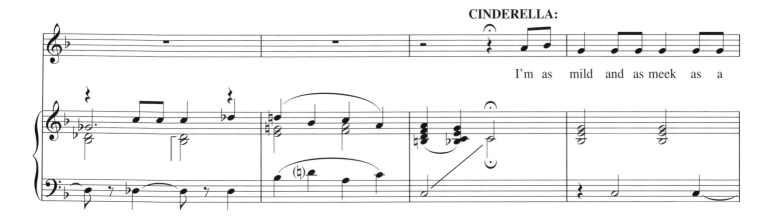

CINDERELLA:

I'm as mild and as meek as a

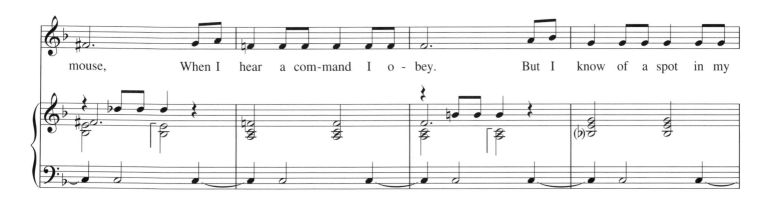

mouse, When I hear a com-mand I o-bey. But I know of a spot in my

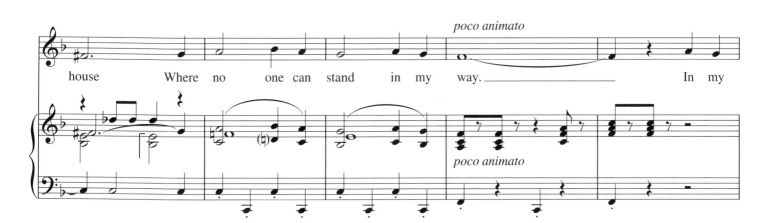

house Where no one can stand in my way. _____ In my

poco animato

Copyright © 1957 by Richard Rodgers and Oscar Hammerstein II
Copyright Renewed
WILLIAMSON MUSIC owner of publication and allied rights throughout the world
International Copyright Secured   All Rights Reserved

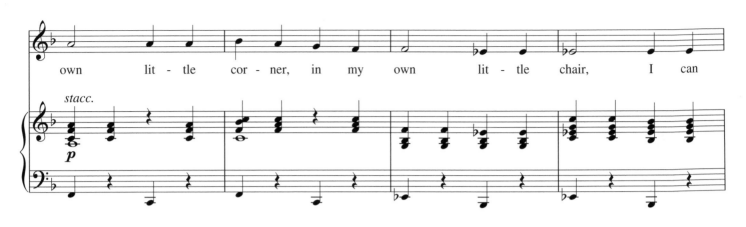

own lit - tle cor - ner, in my own lit - tle chair, I can

be what - ev - er I want to be._____ On the

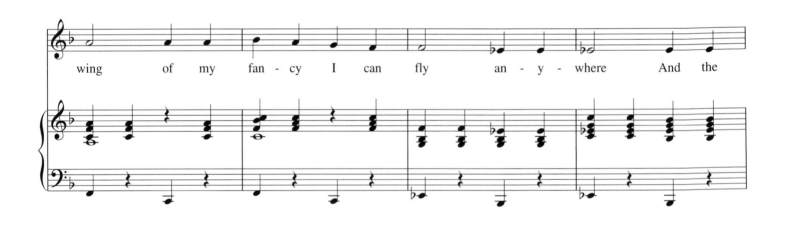

wing of my fan - cy I can fly an - y - where And the

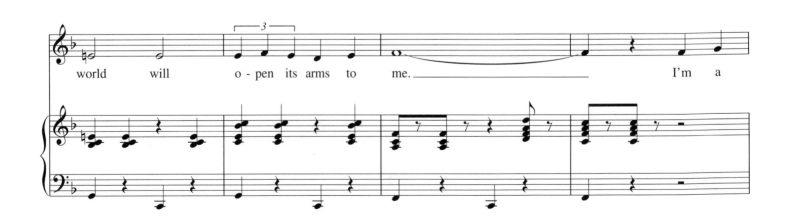

world will o - pen its arms to me._____ I'm a

young Nor - we - gian prin - cess or a milk maid,_____ I'm the

great - est pri - ma don - na in Mi - lan,_____ I'm an

heir - ess who has al - ways had her silk made_____ By her

own flock of silk - worms in Ja - pan!_____ I'm a

34

hunt - ress on an Af - ri - can sa - fa - ri _____ (It's a

dang - 'rous type of sport and yet it's fun); _____ In the

night I sal - ly forth to seek my quar - ry, _____ And I

find I for - got to bring my gun! _____ I am

TEN MINUTES AGO

from *Cinderella*

Lyrics by OSCAR HAMMERSTEIN II
Music by RICHARD RODGERS

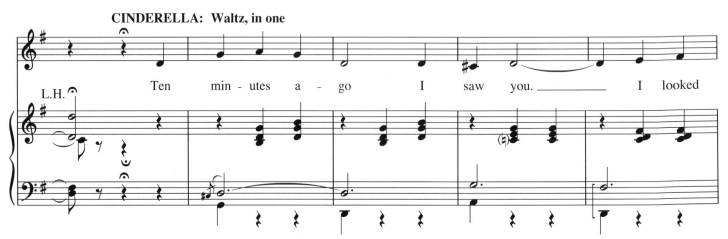

The song is sung twice in the show, first by the Prince, then by Cinderella.

Copyright © 1957 by Richard Rodgers and Oscar Hammerstein II
Copyright Renewed
WILLIAMSON MUSIC owner of publication and allied rights throughout the world
International Copyright Secured   All Rights Reserved

O - ver moun - tain and mead - ow and glen, _____ And I like it so

well that for all I can tell I may nev - er come down a - gain! _____ I may

1.

nev - er come down to earth a - gain. _____

2.

In the gain! _____

IF I LOVED YOU

from *Carousel*

Lyrics by OSCAR HAMMERSTEIN II
Music by RICHARD RODGERS

Copyright © 1945 by WILLIAMSON MUSIC
Copyright Renewed
International Copyright Secured   All Rights Reserved

tan - gle in the threads, And the warp - 'd get mixed with the woof___

___ If I loved you

But

Broadly

some - how I can see just ex - act - ly how I'd be.

Moderato espressivo

If I loved you, Time___ and a - gain___ I would try to say

ART IS CALLING FOR ME

from *The Enchantress*

Music by VICTOR HERBERT
Lyrics by HARRY B. SMITH

Copyright © 2010 by HAL LEONARD CORPORATION
International Copyright Secured All Rights Reserved

hate it all, _____ and I show it. *8va* _ _ _ _ _ _ _ _ _ _ _ _ To
burn with lyr - ic am - bi - tion.

sing on the stage, that's the one life for me, My
ten - ors so sweet, if they made love to me, I'd

fig - ure's just like Te - traz - zi - ni; _____ I
be a suc - cess, that I do know; _____ And

know I'd win fame if I sang in "Bo - hème;" That
Mel - ba I'd oust If I once sang in "Faust," That

don - na, don - na, don - na, I I long to shine up - on the
don - na, don - na, don - na, I I long to shine up - on the

stage, _____ I have the em - bon - point to be and
stage, _____ *8va* With my av - oir - du - pois and my

come a queen of song; And my fig - ure would look pret - ty as a
tra la la la la, I would be the chief sen - sa - tion of the

page. _____ I want to be a screech - y,
age. _____ I long to hear them shout - ing:

50

* treechy
** optional lyric: "Songbirds" replacing "plump girls"

TAKE ME TO THE WORLD
from The TV Production *Evening Primrose*

Words and Music by
STEPHEN SONDHEIM

Moderato ma poco rubato (♩ = 80)

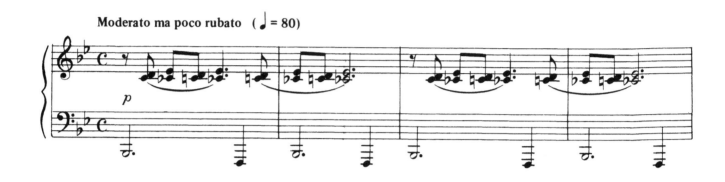

Let me see the world _____ with clouds, Take me to the world. _____

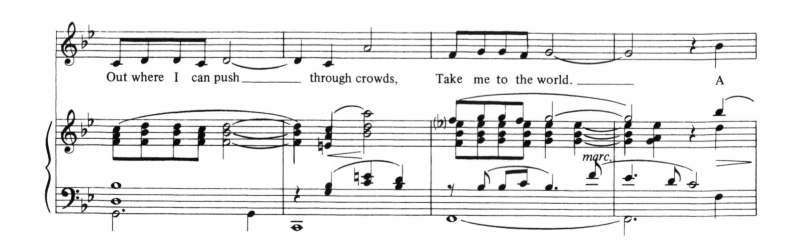

Out where I can push _____ through crowds, Take me to the world. _____ A

Copyright © 1966 by Stephen Sondheim Music and Burthen Music Company, Inc. Owner of allied rights throughout the world
Copyright Renewed
Chappell & Co. sole selling agent
International Copyright Secured   All Rights Reserved

We shall have the world. _____ I'll hold your hand And

know I'm not a - lone. We shall have the world _____ to keep,

Such a love-ly world _____ we'll weep. We shall have the world for - ev - er for our

own. _____

MATCHMAKER
from the Musical *Fiddler on the Roof*

Words by SHELDON HARNICK
Music by JERRY BOCK

This trio for Hodel, Chava and Tzeitel has been adapted as a solo.

Copyright © 1964 Bock IP LLC and Mayerling Productions, Ltd.
Copyright Renewed 1992
All Rights for Mayerling Productions, Ltd. Administered by R&H Music
International Copyright Secured   All Rights Reserved

58

schol - ar. For Ma - ma, make him rich as a king. For

me, well— I would-n't hol - ler if he were as

hand - some as an - y - thing! _____ Match-mak - er, match-mak - er,

cresc.

mf

p

make me a match. Find me a find; Catch me a

catch.   Night af -- ter night in the dark I'm a -- lone,   so

find me a match   of   my   own. _____

Optional ending

pp   *mf*

Continuing to second verse

own. _____

mf   *poco rit.*   Slower (still in 1)

poco rit.

pp

[This interlude represents Tzeitel's cut section, raising worry over possible bad matches. The actor should shift from bright

hope to worry and alarm.] **Allegro**

[Tempo primo]

Match - mak - er,

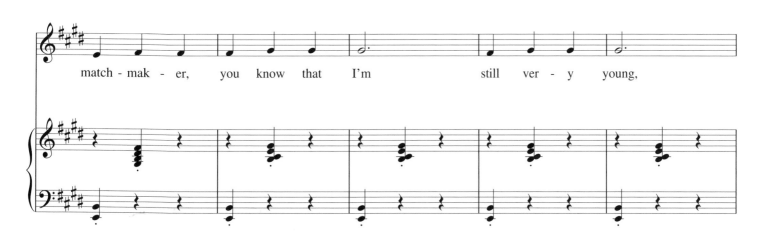

match - mak - er,   you   know   that   I'm   still   ver - y   young,

Please— take your time! Up to this min - ute I mis - un - der -

stood that I could get stuck for good! _____ Dear

Yen - te, see that he's gen - tle. Re - mem -

ber, you were al - so a bride. It's not— that—

I'm sen - ti - men - tal, it's just that I'm ter - ri -

fied! _____ Match-mak - er, match-mak - er,

plan me no plans. I'm in no rush. May - be I've

learned: Play - ing with match - es a girl can get burned. So

bring me no ring. Groom me no groom. Find me no

find. Catch me no catch, un - less he's a

match - less match! _____

FAR FROM THE HOME I LOVE
from the Musical *Fiddler on the Roof*

Words by SHELDON HARNICK
Music by JERRY BOCK

Copyright © 1964 Bock IP LLC and Mayerling Productions, Ltd.
Copyright Renewed 1992
All Rights for Mayerling Productions, Ltd. Administered by R&H Music
International Copyright Secured   All Rights Reserved

Close to the peo-ple who are close to me, Here in the home I love.

Più mosso

Who could see that a man would come Who would change the shape of my dreams?

L.H.

rit.

Meno mosso-In 4

Help-less now, I stand with him, Watch-ing old-er dreams grow dim.

p

poco rit.

In 2

Oh, what a mel-an-chol-y choice this is, Want-ing home, want-ing him.

MUCH MORE
from *The Fantasticks*

Words by TOM JONES
Music by HARVEY SCHMIDT

Moderately - with spirit ♩ = 160

Copyright © 1960 by Tom Jones and Harvey Schmidt
Copyright Renewed
Chappell & Co. owner of publication and allied rights throughout the world
International Copyright Secured   All Rights Reserved

store, But I want much more than keep-ing house! Much

more! Much more! Much _

more!

I'LL KNOW
from *Guys and Dolls*

By FRANK LOESSER

Adapted as a solo here, the song is a duet scene for Sarah and Sky in the show.

© 1950 (Renewed) FRANK MUSIC CORP.
All Rights Reserved

run to his arms that at last I've come home safe and sound and till

(with mounting determination)

then I shall wait and till then I'll be

strong for I'll know when my love comes a - long.

I won't take a chance, my

love will be just what I need not some fly - by - night Broad - way ro -

mance, and till then I shall wait and till

then _____ I'll be strong _____ for I'll know when my

love _____ comes a - long. _____

ON THE STEPS OF THE PALACE
from *Into the Woods*

Words and Music by
STEPHEN SONDHEIM

© 1988 RILTING MUSIC, INC.
All Rights Administered by WB MUSIC CORP.
All Rights Reserved   Used by Permission

82

For ex - am - ple, a shoe. And then see what he'll do.

Now it's he and not you who is stuck with a shoe, In a stew, In the goo,

cresc.

And you've learned some - thing, too, Some - thing you nev - er knew, _____

mf

On the steps of the pal - ace. _____

CHILDREN WILL LISTEN
from *Into the Woods*

Words and Music by
STEPHEN SONDHEIM

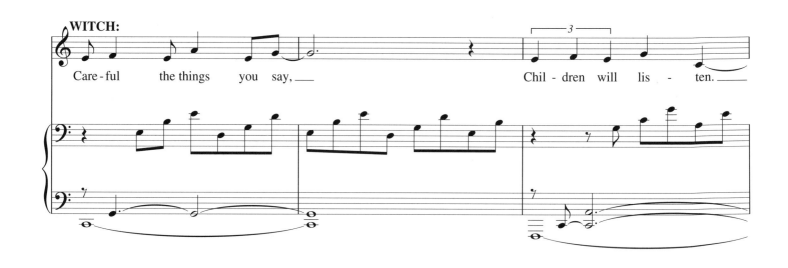

This song is an ensemble number in the show, adapted as a solo for this edition.

© 1988 RILTING MUSIC, INC.
All Rights Administered by WB MUSIC CORP.
All Rights Reserved Used By Permission

IN HIS EYES

from the Broadway Musical *Jekyll & Hyde*

Words by LESLIE BRICUSSE
Music by FRANK WILDHORN

This is a duet in the show.

Copyright © 1995 Stage And Screen Music, Ltd. (BMI), Cherry Lane Music Publishing Company, Inc. (ASCAP),
Scaramanga Music, Inc. (ASCAP) and State One Songs
Worldwide Rights for Stage And Screen Music, Ltd. Administered by Cherry River Music Co.
Worldwide Rights for Scaramanga Music, Inc. and State One Songs America Administered by Cherry Lane Music Publishing Company, Inc.
International Copyright Secured   All Rights Reserved

I WHISTLE A HAPPY TUNE

from *The King and I*

Lyrics by OSCAR HAMMERSTEIN II
Music by RICHARD RODGERS

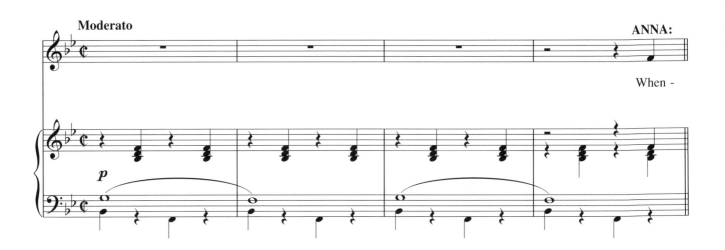

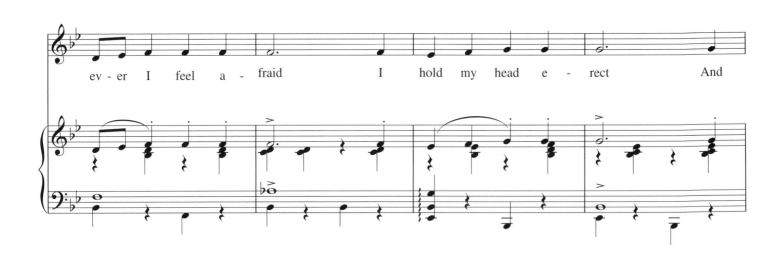

Copyright © 1951 by Richard Rodgers and Oscar Hammerstein II
Copyright Renewed
WILLIAMSON MUSIC owner of publication and allied rights throughout the world
International Copyright Secured   All Rights Reserved

peo - ple I fear I fool my - self as well! I whis - tle a hap - py

tune And ev - 'ry sin - gle time The hap - pi - ness in the

tune con - vin - ces me that I'm not a - fraid.

Make be - lieve you're brave And the trick will take you far.

You may be as brave as you make be-lieve you are.

Whistle

You may be as brave as you make be-lieve you

are.

cresc.

8va

ff *f*

I HAVE DREAMED
from *The King and I*

Lyrics by OSCAR HAMMERSTEIN II
Music by RICHARD RODGERS

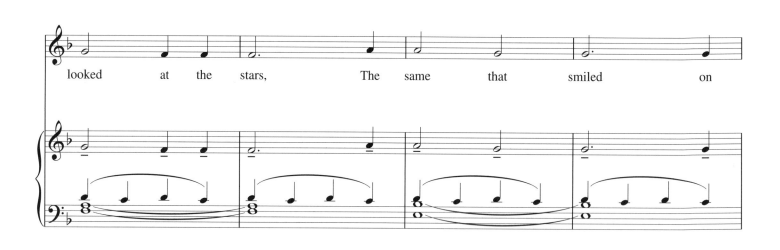

This song is a duet for Tuptim and Lun Tha in the show, adapted as a solo for this edition.

Copyright © 1951 by Richard Rodgers and Oscar Hammerstein II
Copyright Renewed
WILLIAMSON MUSIC owner of publication and allied rights throughout the world
International Copyright Secured   All Rights Reserved

IN MY LIFE

from *Les Misérables*

Music by CLAUDE-MICHEL SCHÖNBERG
Lyrics by ALAIN BOUBLIL, JEAN-MARC NATEL
and HERBERT KRETZMER

This song for Cosette, Valjean, Marius and Eponine previously adapted as a solo.

Music and Lyrics Copyright © 1980 by Editions Musicales Alain Boublil
English Lyrics Copyright © 1986 by Alain Boublil Music Ltd. (ASCAP)
Mechanical and Publication Rights for the U.S.A. Administered by Alain Boublil Music Ltd. (ASCAP)
c/o Joel Faden & Co., Inc., MLM 250 West 57th St., 26th Floor, New York, NY 10107, Tel. (212) 246-7203, Fax (212) 246-7217, mwlock@joelfaden.com
International Copyright Secured. All Rights Reserved. This music is copyright. Photocopying is illegal.
All Performance Rights Restricted.

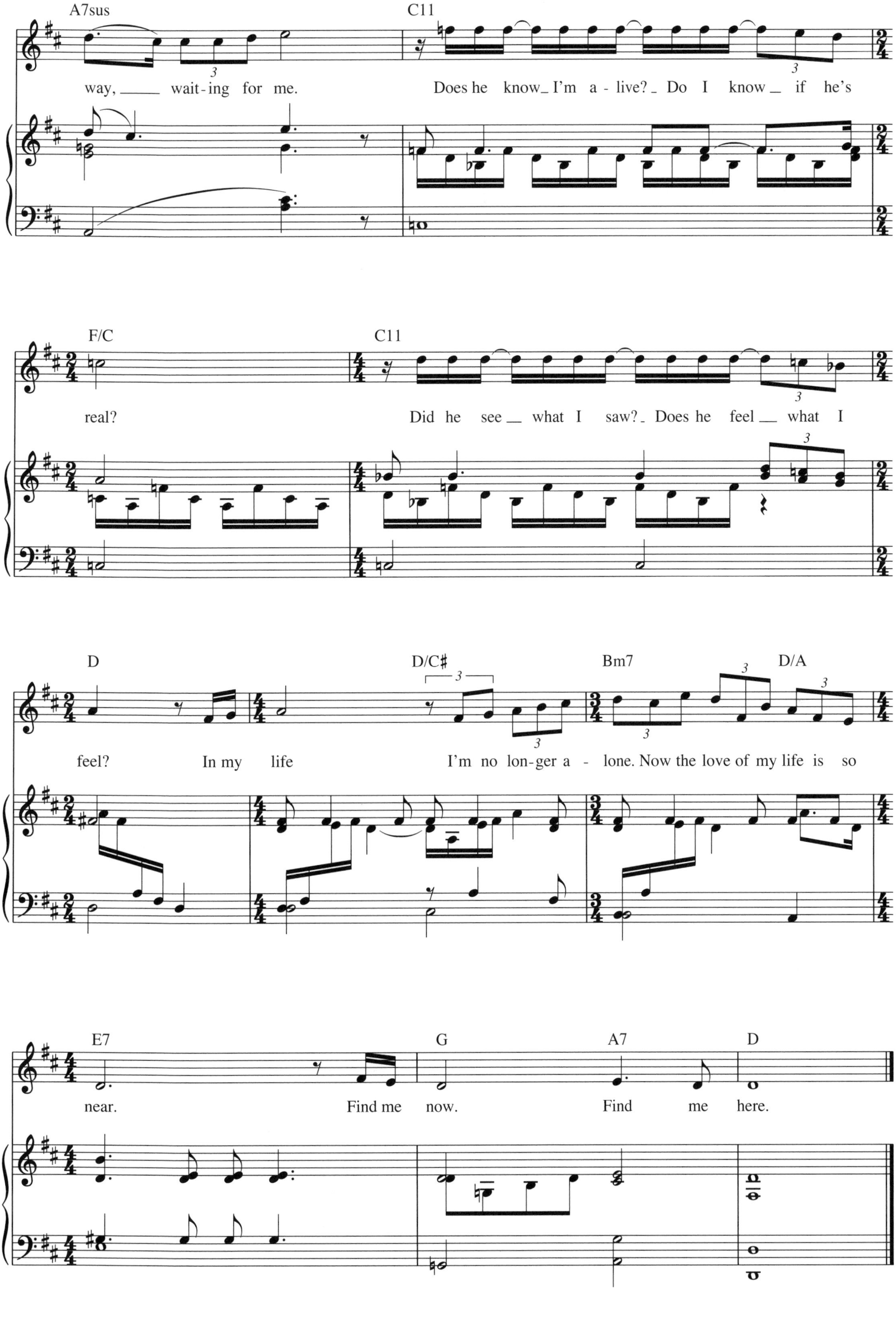
A7sus
C11
way, wait-ing for me.
Does he know I'm a-live? Do I know if he's
F/C
C11
real?
Did he see what I saw? Does he feel what I
D
D/C♯
Bm7
D/A
feel? In my life I'm no lon-ger a-lone. Now the love of my life is so
E7
G
A7
D
near. Find me now. Find me here.

THE BEAUTY IS
from *The Light in the Piazza*

Words and Music by
ADAM GUETTEL

Copyright © 2005 MATTHEW MUSIC
Publishing and Allied Rights Administered by WILLIAMSON MUSIC throughout the world
International Copyright Secured   All Rights Reserved

It's the land of na - ked mar - ble boys! ___

Some - thing we don't see a lot in Win - ston Sa - lem.

That's the land of cor - du - roys! ___

Poco più mosso, flowing, but exact tempo

I'm just a some-one in an

mf

old mu - se - um. Far a - way from home as some-one can go.

And the beau - ty is I still meet peo - ple I know. ___ Hel -

Expressively

lo. This is want-ing some-thing. This is reach-ing for it.

This is wish-ing that a mo-ment would ar - rive. This is tak - ing chanc - es.

in It - a - ly. Ev - ery-one's a fa - ther or

a son. ___ I think if I had a child ___

I would take such care of her. ___ Then I would - n't

feel like one. ___ I've

hard-ly met a sin-gle soul, but I am not a-lone._____ I feel

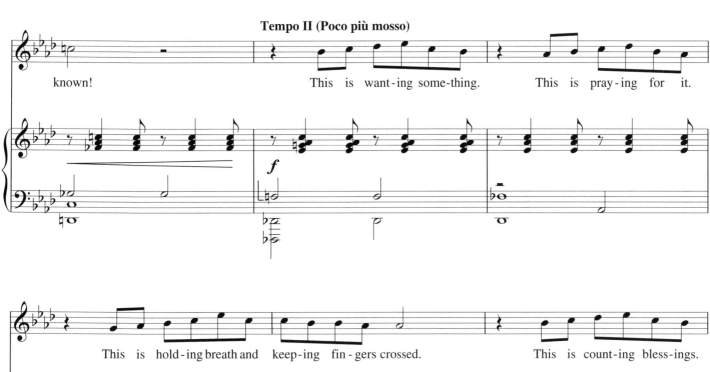

Tempo II (Poco più mosso)

known! This is want-ing some-thing. This is pray-ing for it.

This is hold-ing breath and keep-ing fin-gers crossed. This is count-ing bless-ings.

This is won-d'ring when I'll see that__ boy a-gain.__

THE GLAMOROUS LIFE
from the film version of *A Little Night Music*

Words and Music by
STEPHEN SONDHEIM

© 1973 (Renewed) RILTING MUSIC, INC.
All Rights Administered by WB MUSIC CORP.
All Rights Reserved   Used by Permission

Mend the clothes and tend the chil - dren. Or - din-ar - y moth - ers, like

or - din-ar - y wives, Make the beds and

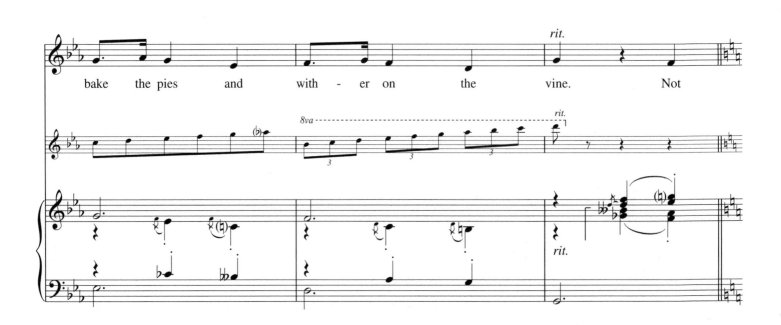

bake the pies and with - er on the vine. Not

tain - ing   their   poise.

Sand - wich - es   on - ly,   but   she   eats   what   she

wants   when   she   wants.

Some - times   it's   lone - ly, _____   but   she   meets   man - y

hand - some gal - lants.

Or - din - ar - y moth-ers don't live out of cas - es But

Or - din - ar - y moth-ers don't go dif - f'rent plac - es, Which

or - din - ar - y moth-ers can't do, Be - ing moth - ers all

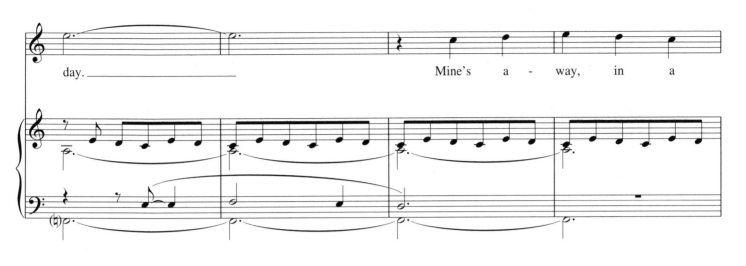

day. _____ Mine's a - way, in a

play _____ And she's real - er than

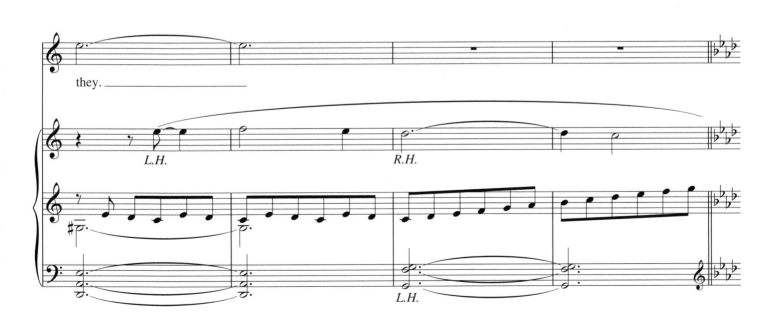

they. _____

120

SOME THINGS ARE MEANT TO BE

from the Stage Musical *Little Women*

Music by JASON HOWLAND
Lyrics by MINDI DICKSTEIN

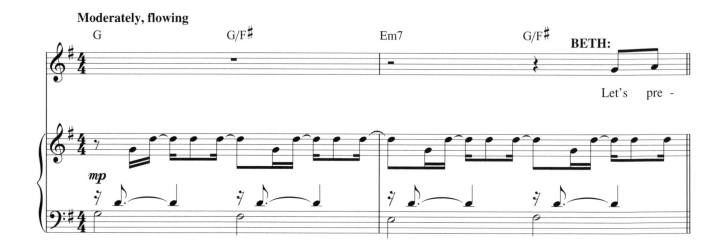

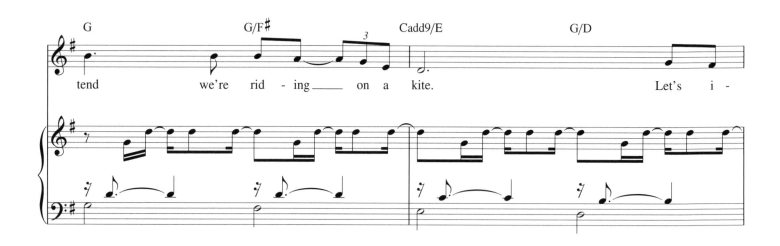

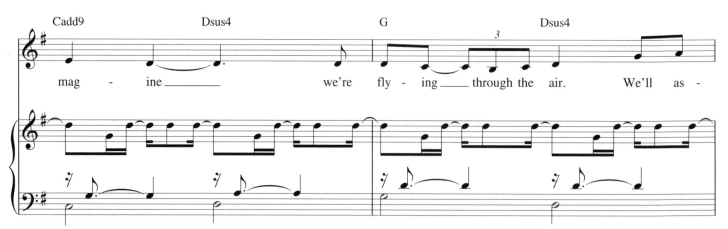

This duet for Beth and Jo is adapted as a solo.

Copyright © 2005 Cherry River Music Co. (BMI), Howland Music (BMI) and Little Esky Publishing (ASCAP)
Worldwide Rights for Howland Music Administered by Cherry River Music Co.
Worldwide Rights for Little Esky Publishing Administered by Cherry Lane Music Publishing Company, Inc.
International Copyright Secured   All Rights Reserved

130

133

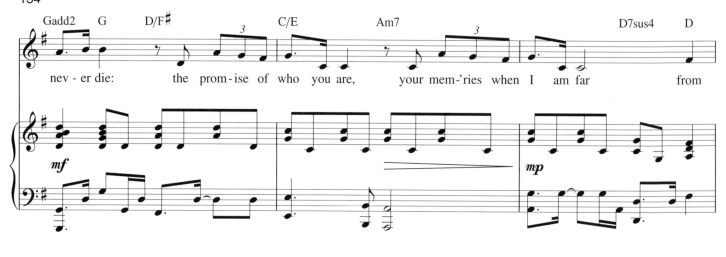

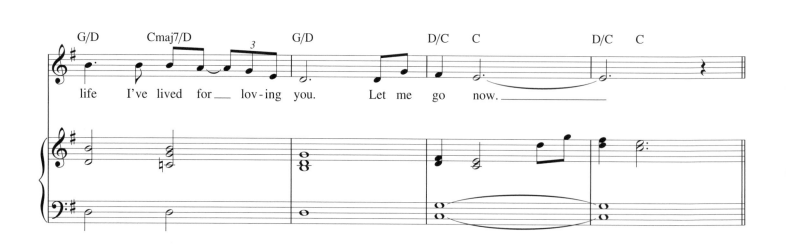

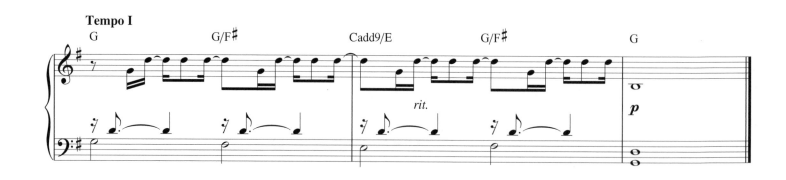

WOULDN'T IT BE LOVERLY

from *My Fair Lady*

Words by ALAN JAY LERNER
Music by FREDERICK LOEWE

Moderato

pp leggiero

ELIZA:

All I want is a room some-where; Far a-way from the cold night air. With one e-nor-mous chair; oh, would-n't it be lov-er-ly? Lots of choc'-late for me to eat; Lots of coal ma-kin'

Copyright © 1956 by Alan Jay Lerner and Frederick Loewe
Copyright Renewed
Chappell & Co. owner of publication and allied rights throughout the world
International Copyright Secured   All Rights Reserved

I COULD HAVE DANCED ALL NIGHT

from *My Fair Lady*

Words by ALAN JAY LERNER
Music by FREDERICK LOEWE

Copyright © 1956 by Alan Jay Lerner and Frederick Loewe
Copyright Renewed
Chappell & Co. owner of publication and allied rights throughout the world
International Copyright Secured   All Rights Reserved

could - n't sleep to - night!   Not   for   all   the

jew - els in the crown!   I could have

danced   all   night!   I could have danced   all

night!   And   still   have begged   for

140

141

wings And done a thou - sand things I've
nev - er done be - fore.
I'll nev - er know what made it so ex -
cit - ing; Why all at once my

SHOW ME
from *My Fair Lady*

Words by ALAN JAY LERNER
Music by FREDERICK LOEWE

Copyright © 1956 by Alan Jay Lerner and Frederick Loewe
Copyright Renewed
Chappell & Co. owner of publication and allied rights throughout the world
International Copyright Secured   All Rights Reserved

GOODNIGHT, MY SOMEONE
from Meredith Willson's *The Music Man*

By MEREDITH WILLSON

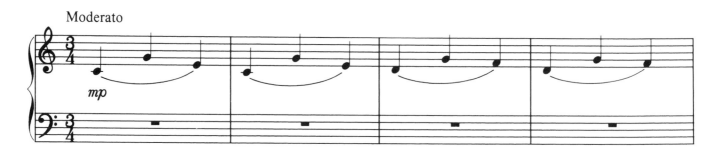

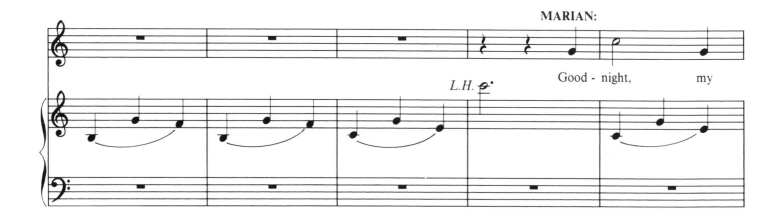

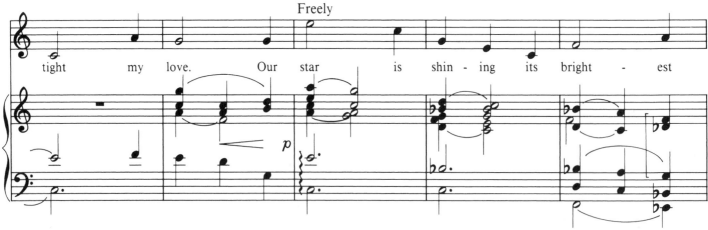

© 1957 (Renewed) FRANK MUSIC CORP. and MEREDITH WILLSON MUSIC
All Rights Reserved

light for good-night, my love, for good-night. _____ Sweet

dreams be yours, dear, if dreams there be; Sweet dreams to

car - ry you close to me. I wish they may, and I

wish they might. Now good-night, my some - one, good - night. _____

L.H.

L.H.

Poco mosso

8va True love can be whis-pered from heart to heart, when

lov-ers are part-ed they say. But I must de-

poco rit.

pend on a wish and a star, as long as my heart does-n't

Tempo I

know who you are. Sweet dreams be yours, dear, if dreams there

SIMPLE LITTLE THINGS

from *110 in the Shade*

Words by TOM JONES
Music by HARVEY SCHMIDT

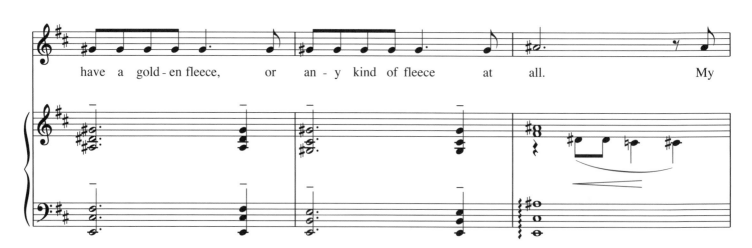

Copyright © 1963 by Tom Jones and Harvey Schmidt
Copyright Renewed
Portfolio Music, Inc., owner, and Chappell & Co., administrator, of publication and allied rights throughout the world
International Copyright Secured   All Rights Reserved

dreams, like my name, are ver - y plain; no shin - ing knight must kneel. My

dreams, like my name, are ver - y plain; but nev - er - the - less, they're

real. They're all so ver - y real.

156

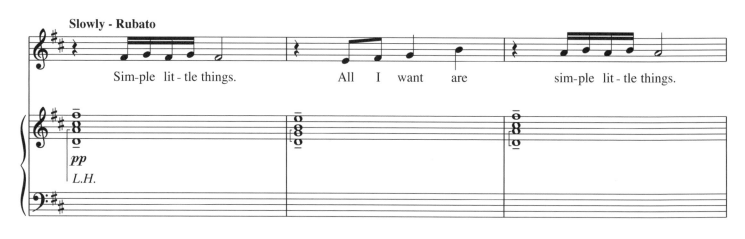

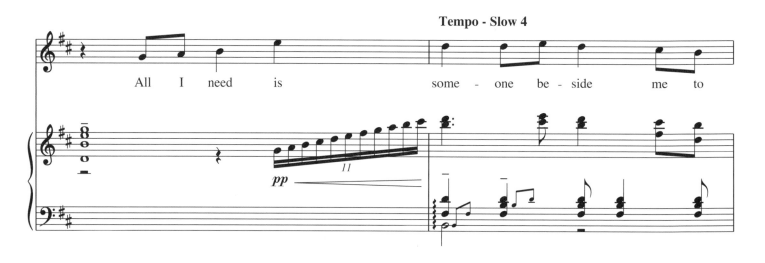

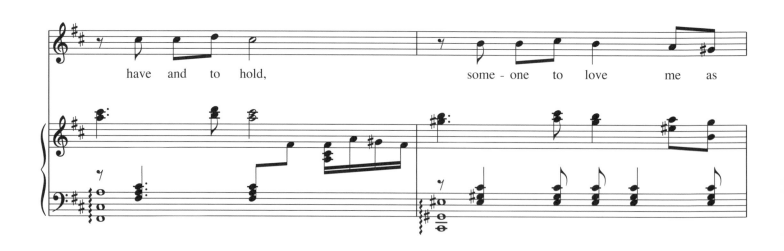

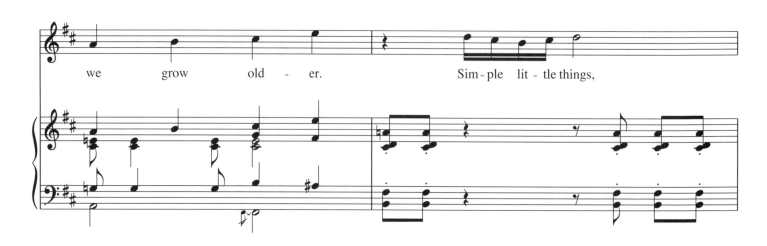

THINK OF ME

from *The Phantom of the Opera*

Music by ANDREW LLOYD WEBBER
Lyrics by CHARLES HART
Additional Lyrics by RICHARD STILGOE

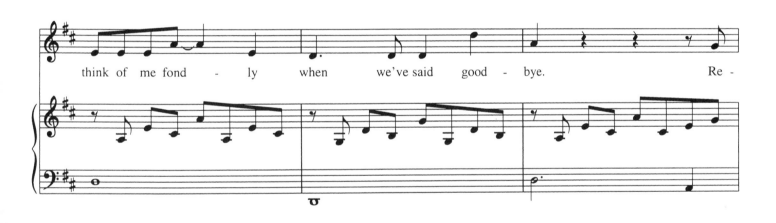

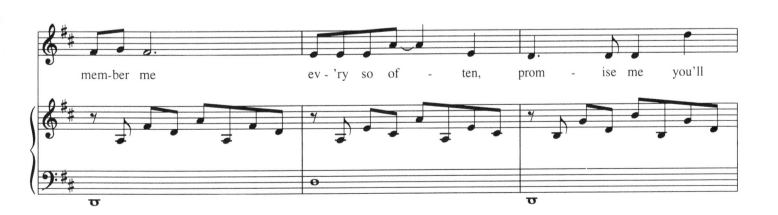

© Copyright 1986 Andrew Lloyd Webber licensed to The Really Useful Group Ltd.
International Copyright Secured   All Rights Reserved

try.

On that day, _____ that not so dis-tant day, _____ when you are

far a - way and free, if you ev - er find a

mo - ment, spare a thought for

me.

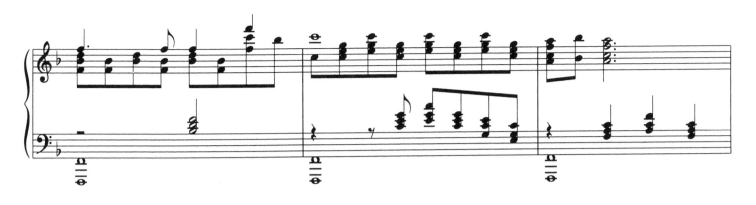

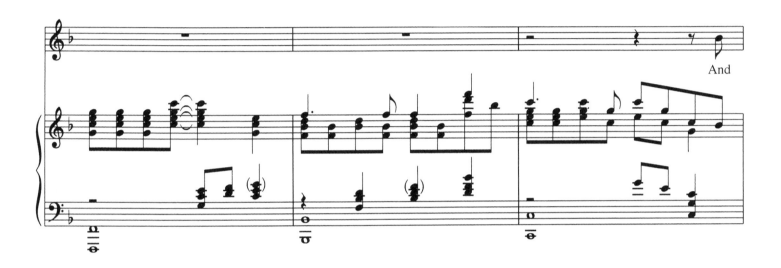

And

though it's clear, though it was al-ways clear___ that this was nev - er meant to

mp

be, if you hap-pen to re - mem - ber,

stop and think of me. Think of

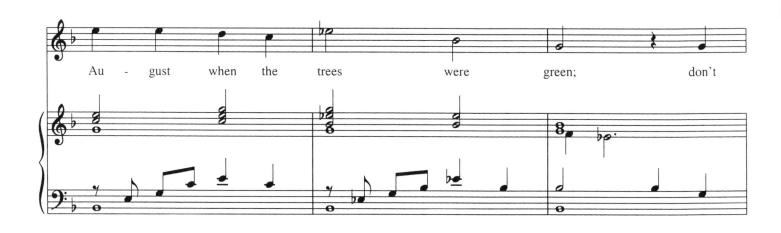

Au - gust when the trees were green; don't

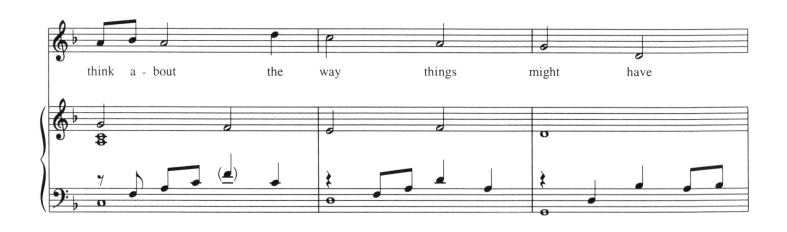

think a - bout the way things might have

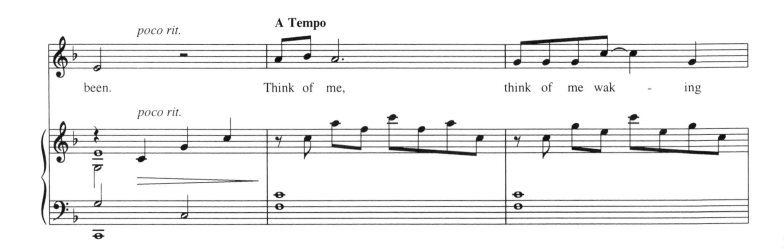

been. Think of me, think of me wak - ing

si - lent and re - signed. I - mag-ine me,

try - ing too hard __ to put you from my mind.

Think of me ___ please say you'll think of me ___ what - ev - er else you choose to

no rit.

do. There will nev - er be a day when

no rit.

WISHING YOU WERE SOMEHOW HERE AGAIN

from *The Phantom of the Opera*

Music by ANDREW LLOYD WEBBER
Lyrics by CHARLES HART
Additional Lyrics by RICHARD STILGOE

© Copyright 1986 Andrew Lloyd Webber licensed to The Really Useful Group Ltd.
International Copyright Secured   All Rights Reserved

cold and mon-u-men-tal, seem for you the wrong com-pan-ions;

rit. *a tempo*

you were warm and gen-tle.

pp a tempo

rit.

Too man-y years fight-ing back tears, why can't the past just

die? Wish-ing you were some-how here a-gain;

ff

know-ing we must say good - bye. Try to for-give,

teach me to live, give me the strength to try. No more

mem-o-ries no more si - lent tears, no more gaz-ing a - cross the wast - ed

years. Help me say good - bye! Help me say good - bye!

IT WONDERS ME

from *Plain and Fancy*

Lyrics by ARNOLD B. HORWITT
Music by ALBERT HAGUE

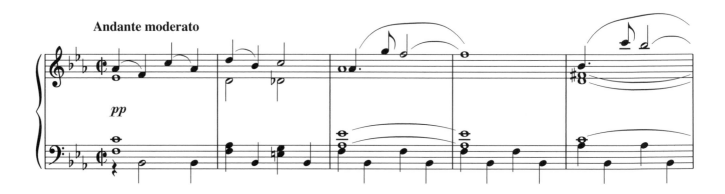

Copyright © 1954 by Chappell & Co.
Copyright Renewed
International Copyright Secured   All Rights Reserved

So won-der-ful sweet the mel-o-dy,

It won-ders me. So green the field,

So blue the sky, So gold the tree,

It won-ders me. *(opt.)*

MAKE BELIEVE
from *Show Boat*

Lyrics by OSCAR HAMMERSTEIN II
Music by JEROME KERN

This song is a duet for Magnolia and Ravenal in the show, adapted as a solo for this edition.

Copyright © 1927 UNIVERSAL - POLYGRAM INTERNATIONAL PUBLISHING, INC.
Copyright Renewed
All Rights Reserved   Used by Permission

mind con - ven - tion's P's and Q's.

If we put our thoughts in prac - tice We can ban-ish all re -

gret, I - mag - in - ing most an - y -

thing we choose. We could

THE SOUND OF MUSIC
from *The Sound of Music*

Lyrics by OSCAR HAMMERSTEIN II
Music by RICHARD RODGERS

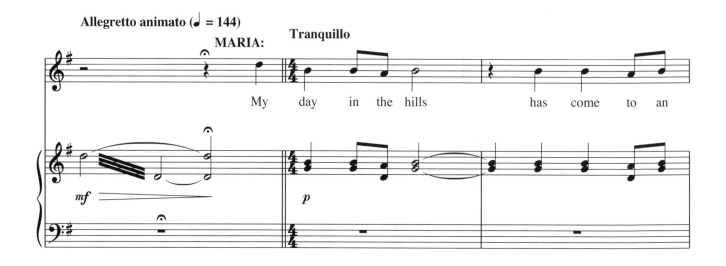

Copyright © 1959 by Richard Rodgers and Oscar Hammerstein II
Copyright Renewed
WILLIAMSON MUSIC owner of publication and allied rights throughout the world
International Copyright Secured   All Rights Reserved

voic - es that urge me to stay. So I pause and I wait and I

lis - ten for one more sound, for one more love - ly thing that the

Con espressione

hills might say. The hills are a - live with the sound of

espr. **p**

mf **p**

mu - sic, _____ with songs they have sung for a thou - sand

years. _____ The hills fill my heart with the sound of

mu - sic. _____ My heart wants to sing ev - 'ry song it

hears. _____ My heart wants to beat like the wings of the birds that rise from the

lake to the trees. My heart wants to sigh like a chime that flies from a

The optional high note is an editorial suggestion for consideration.

I HAVE CONFIDENCE

from *The Sound of Music*

Music and Lyrics by
RICHARD RODGERS

Moderato (rubato)

MARIA:

What will this day be like? I won-der. _ What will my fu-ture

Più mosso

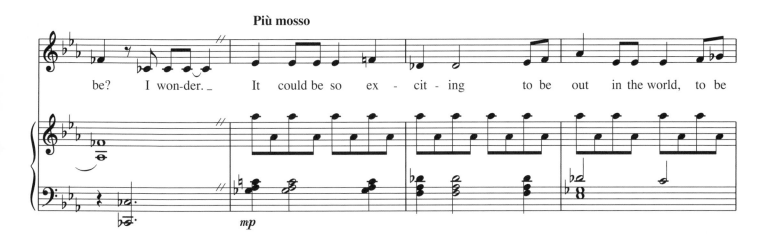

be? I won-der. _ It could be so ex-cit-ing to be out in the world, to be

free. My heart should be wild-ly re-joic-ing. Oh, what's the mat-ter with

Copyright © 1964, 1965 by Richard Rodgers
Copyright Renewed
WILLIAMSON MUSIC owner of publication and allied rights throughout the world
International Copyright Secured   All Rights Reserved

MY FAVORITE THINGS

from *The Sound of Music*

Lyrics by OSCAR HAMMERSTEIN II
Music by RICHARD RODGERS

Copyright © 1959 by Richard Rodgers and Oscar Hammerstein II
Copyright Renewed
WILLIAMSON MUSIC owner of publication and allied rights throughout the world
International Copyright Secured   All Rights Reserved

dress - es with blue sat - in sash - es, Snow - flakes that stay on my

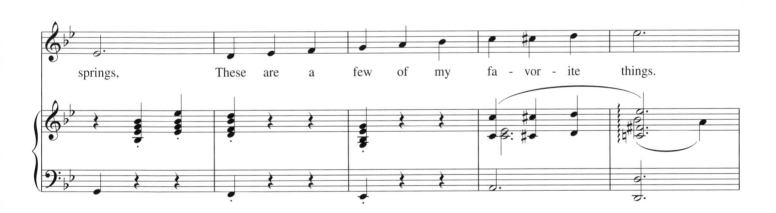

nose and eye - lash - es, Sil - ver white win - ters that melt in - to

springs, These are a few of my fa - vor - ite things.

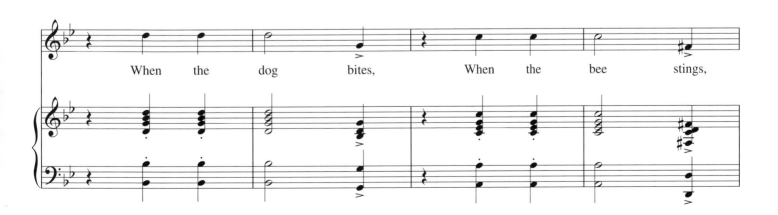

When the dog bites, When the bee stings,

When I'm feel - ing sad, _____ I sim - ply re -

mem - ber my fa - vor - ite things and then I don't feel _____

_____ so bad. _____

p   *f*

sff

I FEEL PRETTY

from *West Side Story*

Lyrics by STEPHEN SONDHEIM
Music by LEONARD BERNSTEIN

This scene for Maria, Francisca, Rosalia and Consuelo has been adapted as a solo for this edition.

Copyright © 1957 by Amberson Holdings LLC and Stephen Sondheim
Copyright Renewed
Leonard Bernstein Music Publishing Company LLC, Publisher
Boosey & Hawkes, Inc., Sole Agent
Copyright For All Countries All Rights Reserved

See the pret-ty girl in that mir-ror there: ___ Who can that at-

trac-tive girl be? ___ Such a pret-ty

face, Such a pret-ty dress, Such a pret-ty smile, Such a pret-ty me! ___

I feel stun-ning ___ And en-

tranc - ing, __ Feel like run-ning and danc-ing for joy,

For I'm loved _____ By a pret - ty __ won - der - ful

boy! _____

I feel pret - ty, __ Oh, so

204

dress, Such a pret-ty smile, Such a pret-ty me!

I feel stun-ning And en-tranc-ing, Feel like run-ning and

danc-ing for joy, For I'm loved By a

pret-ty won-der-ful boy!

WHISPERING
from *Spring Awakening*

Music by DUNCAN SHEIK
Lyrics by STEVEN SATER

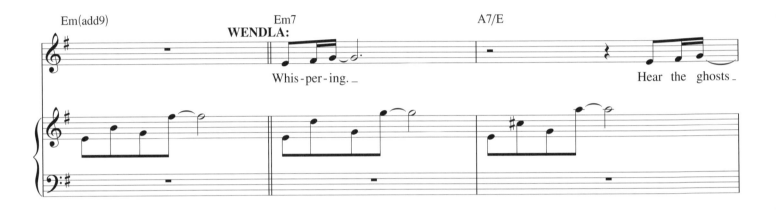

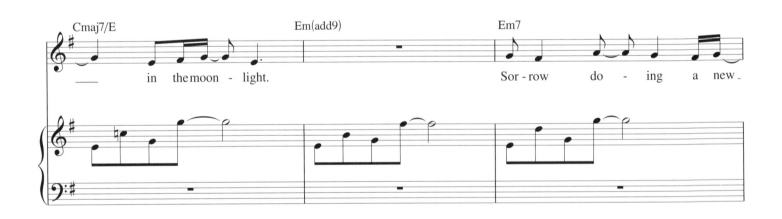

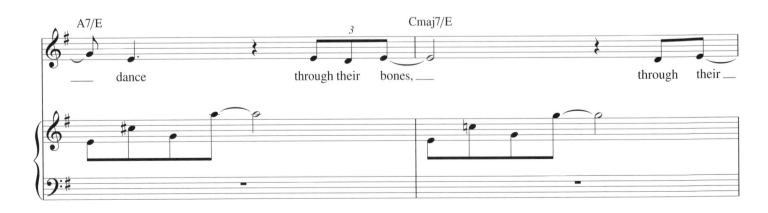

Copyright © 2006 by Universal Music - Careers, Duncan Sheik Songs, Happ Dog Music and Kukuzo Productions, Inc.
All Rights for Duncan Sheik Songs and Happ Dog Music Administered by Universal Music - Careers
International Copyright Secured   All Rights Reserved

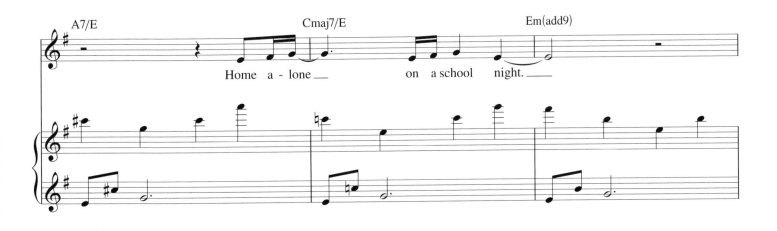

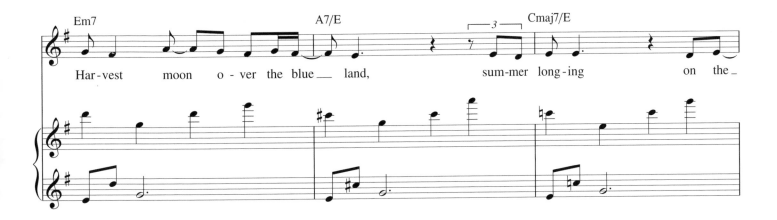

211

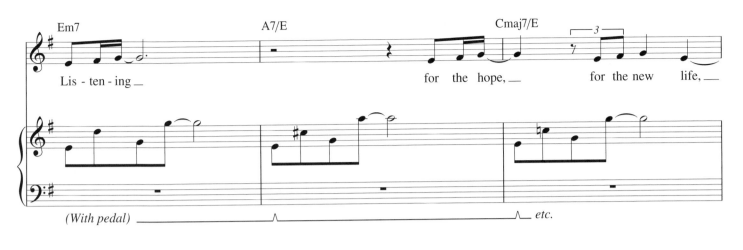

Lis - ten - ing — for the hope, — for the new life, —

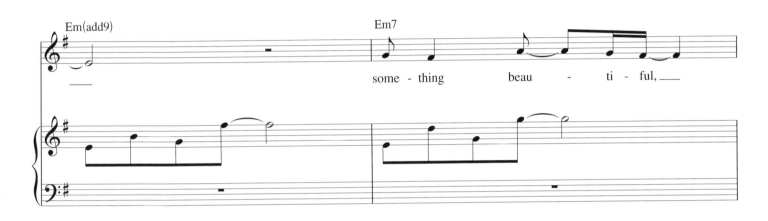

— some - thing beau - ti - ful, —

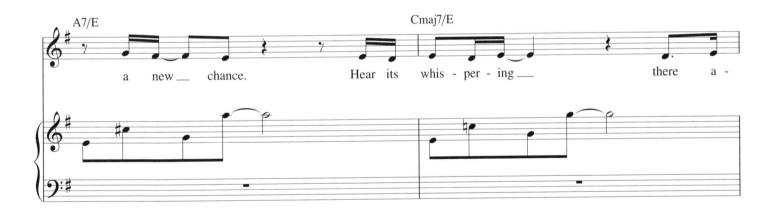

a new — chance. Hear its whis - per - ing — there a -

gain.

GREEN FINCH AND LINNET BIRD

from *Sweeney Todd*

Words and Music by
STEPHEN SONDHEIM

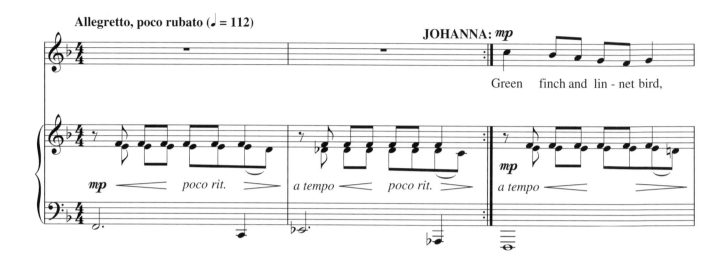

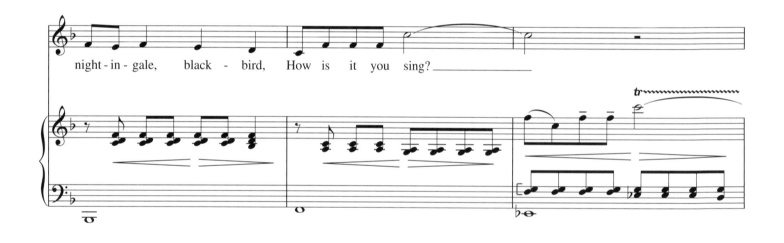

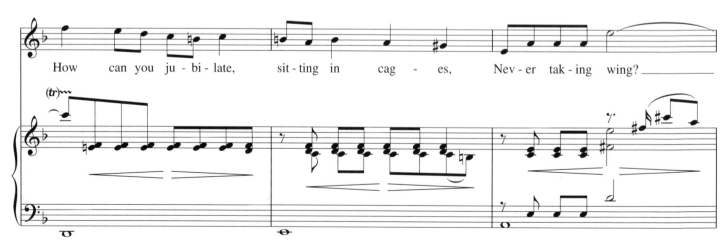

© 1978 RILTING MUSIC, INC.
All Rights Administered by WB MUSIC CORP.
All Rights Reserved   Used by Permission

Out - side the sky waits, beck - on - ing, beck - on - ing.

Just be - yond the bars. How can you re - main, star - ing

at the rain, mad - dened by the stars?

How is it you sing an - y - thing?

POPULAR
from the Broadway Musical *Wicked*

Music and Lyrics by
STEPHEN SCHWARTZ

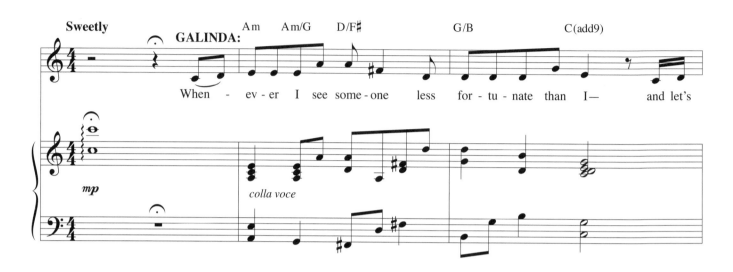

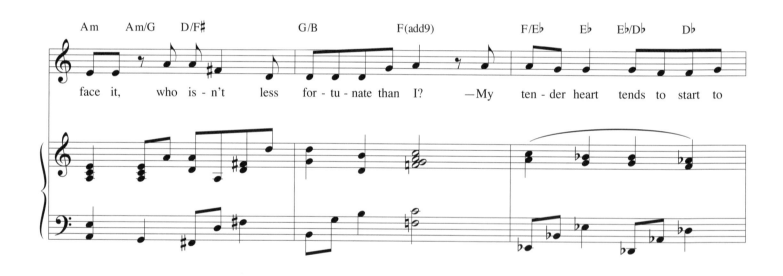

Copyright © 2003 Greydog Music
All Rights Reserved   Used by Permission

A LITTLE BIT IN LOVE
from *Wonderful Town*

Music by LEONARD BERNSTEIN
Lyrics by BETTY COMDEN and ADOLPH GREEN

Copyright © 1953 by Amberson Holdings LLC, Betty Comden and Adolph Green
Copyright Renewed
Chappell & Co. and Leonard Bernstein Music Publishing Company LLC, Publishers
Copyright for All Countries. All Rights Reserved.

haps a lit - tle bit more.

(rhythmically)

When he ___ looks at me, ___ ev - 'ry-thing's ha - zy and all out of fo - cus.

When he ___ touch - es me, ___ I'm in the spell of a strange ho - cus po - cus.

It's so ___ I don't know. ___ I'm so ___ I don't know. ___ I don't